Building Blocks

Written by Claire Owen

My name is Siraj. I live
in the country of Niger,
in West Africa. I am proud
of the interesting mud
buildings of West Africa.
What shape is your home?
What is it made from?

Contents

Made from Mud   4

Amazing Architecture   6

Building Blocks   8

Putting Prisms Together   10

Ancient Pyramids   12

Modern Pyramids   14

The Pyramid Family   16

Living Inside a Circle   18

Cone-Shaped Covers   20

Not-So-Simple Shapes!   22

Sample Answers   24

Index   24

Wherever you see me, you'll find activities to try and questions to answer.

Made from Mud

People in West Africa have constructed huts and houses from mud for thousands of years. As a building material, mud has many advantages. It is easy to work with and readily available. In a hot, dry climate, mud huts are not in danger of being washed away by heavy rain, and they stay cool inside. Best of all, mud is "dirt cheap"!

The Dogon people of Mali, in West Africa, are famous for their villages of mud huts and granaries with flat or thatched roofs.

granary   a building for storing grain

What shapes
make up these West
African buildings?
Can you find a shape
similar to a cube?
... a cone?
... a cylinder?
... a pyramid?

5

Amazing Architecture

Not all of the mud buildings of West Africa are simple huts or houses. The mosque in the city of Djenné, in Mali, is the world's largest mud building. Each spring, after the rainy season has finished, the people of the city help to replaster the mosque with a mixture of mud and rice husks, called *banco*.

mosque   a place of worship for people who follow Islam, the Muslim religion

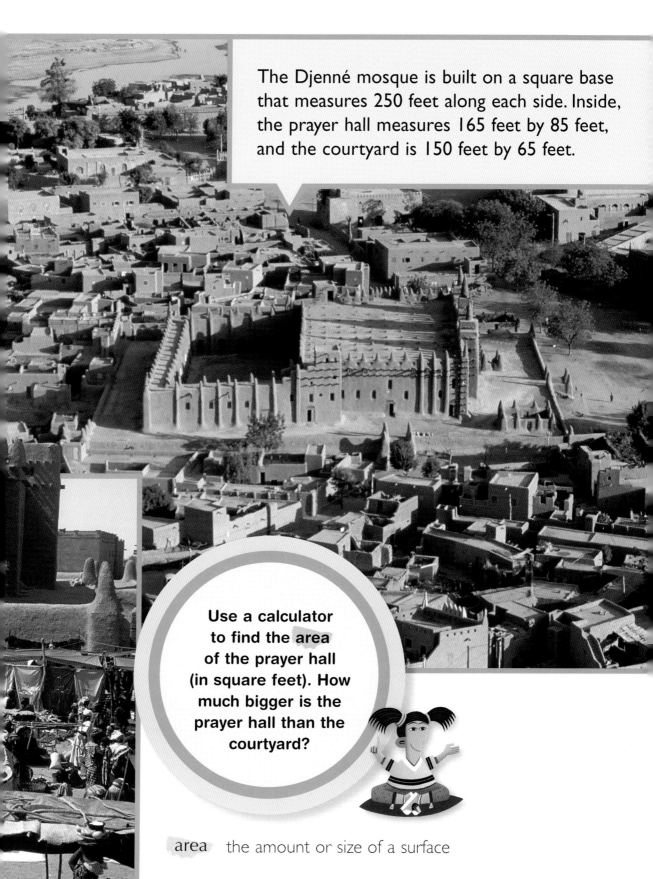

The Djenné mosque is built on a square base that measures 250 feet along each side. Inside, the prayer hall measures 165 feet by 85 feet, and the courtyard is 150 feet by 65 feet.

Use a calculator to find the area of the prayer hall (in square feet). How much bigger is the prayer hall than the courtyard?

area   the amount or size of a surface

Building Blocks

All around the world, people have used geometric shapes as the building blocks for houses, public buildings, and bridges. These building blocks include three-dimensional (3-D) shapes such as pyramids, cones, cylinders, prisms, and even spheres. Some buildings have a simple design based on just one shape. Other buildings have several shapes joined together.

La Defense Dome, Paris, France

geometric shapes 2-D or 3-D shapes such as rectangles, triangles, or prisms

Rectangular prisms are often used as building blocks. These rectangular prisms are made from ice.

St. Paul Ice Palace,
St. Paul, Minnesota

Figure It Out

1. Pick one of the 3-D shapes below. What is it called? How many faces, edges, and vertices does it have?

2. Pick two of the 3-D shapes. How are the shapes alike? How are they different?

3. Which of the 3-D shapes above is your favorite? Where might you see that shape in everyday life?

vertex   (plural *vertices*) a corner point of a triangle, square, cube, or other shape with straight edges

Putting Prisms Together

Many of today's buildings are made up of rectangular prisms, or "box shapes." However, prisms also come in many other shapes. Each prism is named after the shape of its base. A 3-D shape with triangles for the base and the top, joined with rectangles, is called a *triangular prism*. Some prisms have special names. A rectangular prism with six congruent faces is called a *cube*.

congruent   identical in size and shape

Rotterdam, Netherlands (above);
The Pentagon, Arlington, Virginia (below)

What prism shapes can you see in the buildings on this page?

NEC Supertower, Tokyo, Japan

Loretto Inn, Santa Fe, New Mexico

11

Ancient Pyramids

The world's most famous pyramids are at Giza, in Egypt. The pyramids were built more than 4,500 years ago as tombs, or burial places, for Egyptian kings. The Great Pyramid of Khufu is the largest, although it does not always appear so in photos. One of the Seven Wonders of the Ancient World, Khufu's pyramid was the tallest structure on Earth for more than 43 centuries.

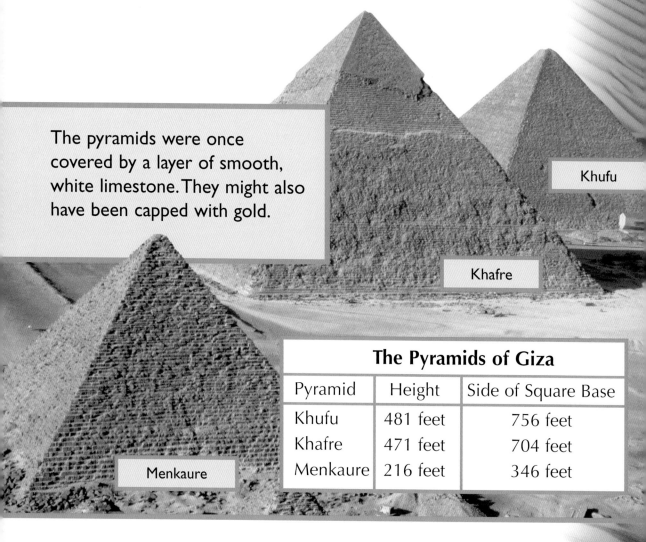

The pyramids were once covered by a layer of smooth, white limestone. They might also have been capped with gold.

Khufu

Khafre

Menkaure

The Pyramids of Giza		
Pyramid	Height	Side of Square Base
Khufu	481 feet	756 feet
Khafre	471 feet	704 feet
Menkaure	216 feet	346 feet

Construct a Pyramid

To construct a pyramid, you will need a piece of card stock, a ruler, a pencil, a pair of scissors, a safety compass, and some tape.

1. In the center of your card, draw a square with $2\frac{1}{2}$ inch sides. (Use something with a square corner to help.) Label two corners A and B.

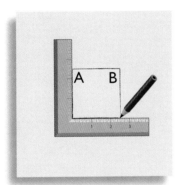

2. Set a safety compass to 3 inches. Place the point on corner A. Use a pencil to draw part of a circle.

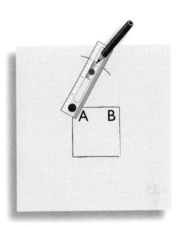

3. Repeat from corner B. Where the curves cross is point C. Draw a line from A to C and another from B to C.

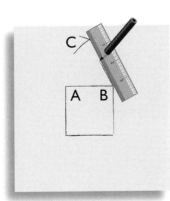

4. Repeat steps 2–3 on the other sides of the square. Cut out the net, fold along each line, and tape the edges together.

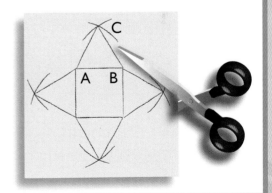

net a 2-D diagram that can be folded up to make a 3-D shape

Modern Pyramids

Modern-day architects have continued to make use of the pyramid. For example, a glass pyramid was built as an entrance to the famous Louvre Museum in Paris, France. In Edmonton, Canada, the Muttart Conservatory has three pyramid-shaped greenhouses. Each greenhouse has a different climate so that visitors can see plants from different parts of the world.

The glass pyramid outside the Louvre Museum was completed in 1989. Below the outdoor pyramid is an upside-down pyramid (right) above a small pyramid!

architect   a person who plans and designs buildings

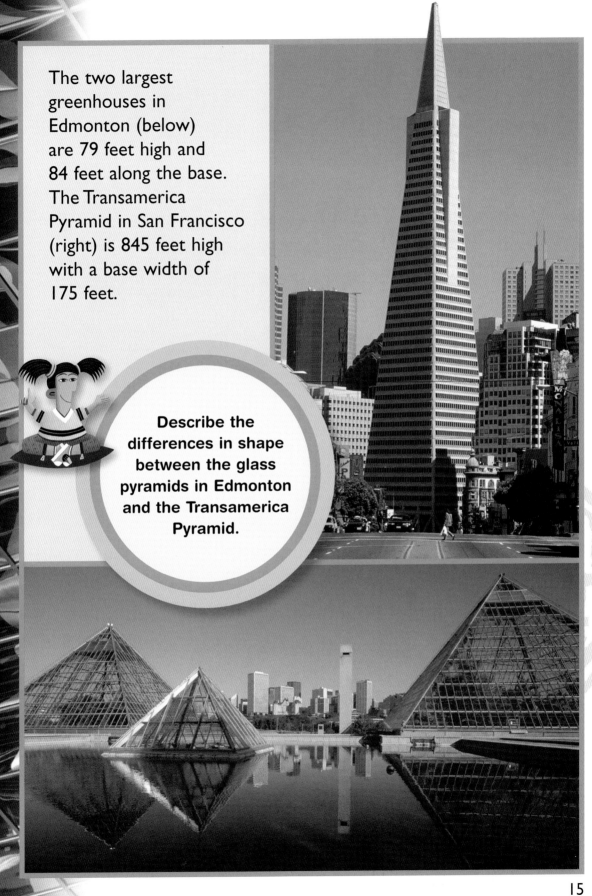

The two largest greenhouses in Edmonton (below) are 79 feet high and 84 feet along the base. The Transamerica Pyramid in San Francisco (right) is 845 feet high with a base width of 175 feet.

Describe the differences in shape between the glass pyramids in Edmonton and the Transamerica Pyramid.

The Pyramid Family

When most people hear the word *pyramid*, they imagine a shape with a square base, similar to the famous pyramids of Giza. However, the base of a pyramid can be a triangle, a hexagon, an octagon, or any other polygon. The base does not have to be regular, and the sides can be slanted at different angles rather than all the same. What a true pyramid must have is a point at the top and flat faces.

These shapes are all pyramids.

regular   describing a shape that has equal sides and equal angles

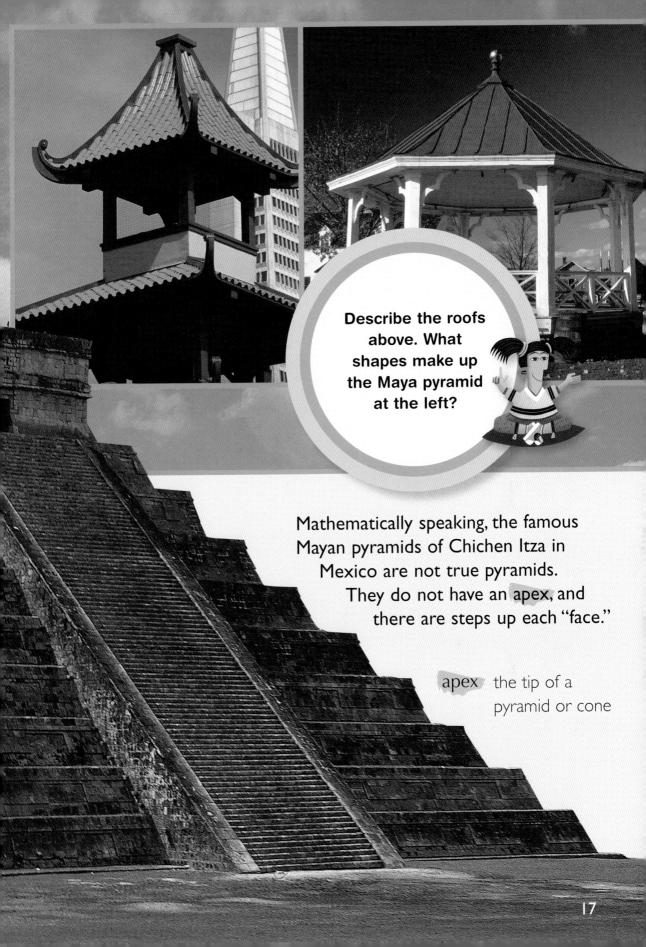

Describe the roofs above. What shapes make up the Maya pyramid at the left?

Mathematically speaking, the famous Mayan pyramids of Chichen Itza in Mexico are not true pyramids. They do not have an apex, and there are steps up each "face."

apex the tip of a pyramid or cone

Living Inside a Circle

What do you think it would be like to live in a round house? What shape would the rooms be? Would the doors and windows be flat or curved? Would the furniture fit neatly against the walls? A house based on a cylinder or a cone could create special challenges for the builder, unless it were a simple, one-room structure.

In the late 1940s, Richard Buckminster Fuller invented the *geodesic dome*—one of the lightest and strongest low-cost buildings ever designed. Geodesic domes are built with triangles, which make the structure strong.

Make a Circular Floor Plan

Create your own floor plan for a circular home. Include a kitchen, bathroom, and other rooms of your choice.

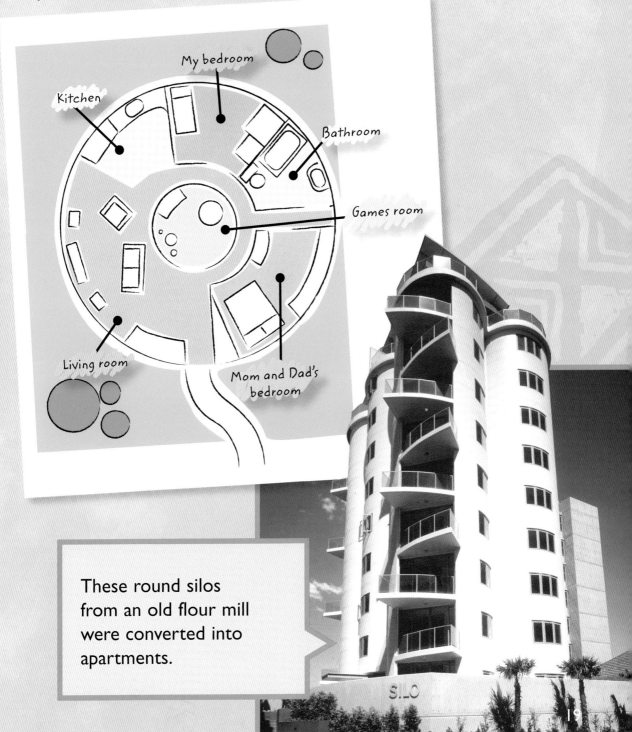

My bedroom

Kitchen

Bathroom

Games room

Living room

Mom and Dad's bedroom

These round silos from an old flour mill were converted into apartments.

SILO

Cone-Shaped Covers

The cone is a natural shape for the roof of a round house. Cone-shaped roofs can be found on many different kinds of buildings, from the mud huts of West Africa to the *trulli* of southern Italy. Trulli are stone houses made up of one or more round rooms. The walls are several feet thick, and the roofs are made from small stones. Some trulli are up to 500 years old.

Trullo House, Italy

Taj Mahal, India

Not many buildings are perfect cylinders, and not many roofs are perfect cones. How would you describe the roofs and buildings on these pages?

Temple of Heaven, Beijing, China (above);
St. Peter's Basilica, Moscow, Russia (right)

Not-So-Simple Shapes!

Not all buildings are based on familiar geometric shapes. Some architects enjoy using new shapes to create unusual-looking buildings. The Spanish architect Antonio Gaudí (1852–1926) used curved walls to give a natural look to buildings. Even today, some of Gaudí's buildings look as if they have come straight out of a fairy tale or a fantasy movie.

Casa Mila is an apartment building designed by Gaudí. It was built with wavy, curved walls.

Sydney Opera House, Australia

Guggenheim Museum,
Bilbao, Spain

How would
you describe the
shapes that make
up the buildings on
these pages?

23

Sample Answers

Page 7 Hall: 14,025 square feet

The hall is 4,275 square feet bigger.

Page 9 1. (See chart below.)

> Make a poster that shows buildings of different shapes. (You could look in magazines or on the Internet for pictures, or you could draw your own.)

Shape	Faces	Edges	Vertices
Cube	6	12	8
Rectangular prism	6	12	8
Cylinder	2	0	0
Cone	1	0	0
Sphere	0	0	0
Hemisphere	1	0	0
Square pyramid	5	8	5
Hexagonal prism	8	18	12

Page 11 Answers might include cubes (top), pentagonal prism (center), rectangular prisms (bottom), rectangular and triangular prisms (right)

Page 17 Roofs: like square-based pyramids; an octagonal pyramid; Maya pyramid: Answers might include "slices" from square-based pyramids and a rectangular prism on the top.

Index

cones   5, 8, 17–18, 20–21

cubes   5, 10

cylinders   5, 8, 18, 21

mud buildings   4, 6–7

prisms   8–11

pyramids   5, 8, 12–17